RAYMOND BRIGGS

Unlucky Wally

TWENTY YEARS ON

SPHERE BOOKS
LIMITED

Also by Raymond Briggs in Sphere Books:

UNLUCKY WALLY

For

LIZ, CLARE & TOM

SPHERE BOOKS LTD
Published by the Penguin Group
27 Wrights Lane, London W8 5TZ, England
Viking Penguin Inc., 40 West 23rd Street, New York, New York 10010, USA
Penguin Books Australia Ltd, Ringwood, Victoria, Australia
Penguin Books Canada Ltd, 2801 John Street, Markham, Ontario, Canada L3R 1B4
Penguin Books (NZ) Ltd, 182-190 Wairau Road, Auckland 10, New Zealand

Penguin Books Ltd, Registered Offices: Harmondsworth, Middlesex, England

First published in Great Britain by Hamish Hamilton Ltd 1989
Published by Sphere Books Ltd 1989

Copyright © 1989 by Raymond Briggs

1 3 5 7 9 10 8 6 4 2

Printed in Italy by
Mondadori Editori, Verona

Twenty years on, Unlucky Wally is still unlucky.

He is still unlucky with his ears, for although they are no bigger, they now look bigger because he has less hair. He is still unlucky with his teeth, as they are all long gone and he now has rows of gleaming NHS plastic. He is still unlucky with his legs, as all the manly hair has fallen out and they now look like sticks of celery.

His nose is still none too good either.

Wally no longer goes on holiday. Eighteen years ago, on a day trip to France, he tried one small bowl of mussels. He quite enjoyed it, but afterwards felt so ill he knew he was going to die that afternoon.

Wally has not been abroad since.

Wally no longer paddles. He is far too old. He was far too old before, but didn't know it. Now he knows it.

Wally no longer swims in lakes. They are much too cold. Occasionally, he used to go to the Municipal Baths where the water was heated, but he is now so self-conscious of his thin and ageing body that he is increasingly reluctant to appear in public undressed.

Besides, on his last visit he contracted a painful verruca on his left foot. It needed four appointments with a Chiropodist to have it removed and these cost over thirty pounds.

Wally has also been discouraged from visiting the Municipal Baths by other unlucky incidents.

Once, when he was watching the swimmers from the balcony, he saw a yellow cloud emanating from a boy standing in the shallow end. For a long time Wally was puzzled by this and it was not until he was half way home on the bus that it dawned on him what it must have been.

Only a week later, Wally was about to climb out when a small dark object bumped against his chest and floated past him. It was sinking as it went and Wally nearly snatched at it to take it out, but something prevented him.

Just then, a little girl next to him let out a shriek, "Mummy! Mummy! Come quickly! Timmy's gone poopy-plops!"

Wally has not been to the Municipal Baths since.

Wally is still a bachelor. Many years ago he was briefly engaged to an older lady called Olive Eggleton. Miss Eggleton had a big chest, a deep voice and three dogs.

One day, she suddenly broke off the engagement and married an even older man who owned a small hotel. Miss Eggleton dropped Wally's engagement ring through his letter box. It was sellotaped to a brief note saying that she had been "swept off her feet by a tycoon."

Wally was not particularly upset. To his own surprise, he found he was quite relieved. He sold the ring and bought himself six months supply of Dubonnet and Lemonade. Wally still daydreams of meeting his childhood sweetheart, Mavis Skinner; but, unknown to Wally, Mavis has been dead for eleven years.

Some years ago, Wally noticed that all the glamorous men in advertisements wore a single ear ring. He thought he would try this, so he had an ear pierced.

Unfortunately, the ear turned septic and soon a thick scab formed with yellow pus oozing from beneath the crust. It was very painful.

Wally gave up the idea of ear rings for good.

When Wally's hair began going grey, he started using a preparation which claimed to restore its natural colour. Wally applied the stuff daily and after a few months his hair was almost chestnut. But, by then, Wally's hair had started falling out with a vengeance and by the time the treatment was complete, most of his hair had gone.

It seems Wally had been right all along to worry about his pendulous testicle. Despite his Doctor's weary reassurances, he continued to worry about it for several years. When at last he mentioned it again, the Doctor examined him and found the testicle would have to be removed.

Wally is now like Adolf Hitler in the World War Two song: "Hitler has only got one ball..."

Wally feels very self-conscious about his condition and in his swimming days he used to stuff a lump of Blu-Tac down his trunks.

As luck would have it, Wally's Mother and Father both died in the same year.

When Wally was called to the hospital for the second time, he found his Mum lying on an iron trolley under a neon light in a sort of annexe. There was a packet of Kleenex and a carton of Vim just by her head. Her jaw had been hastily tied up with gauze and her false teeth stuck out at the wrong angle. Wally had never seen anything so still. When he bent over to kiss her, his nose was running so much it dripped onto her face.

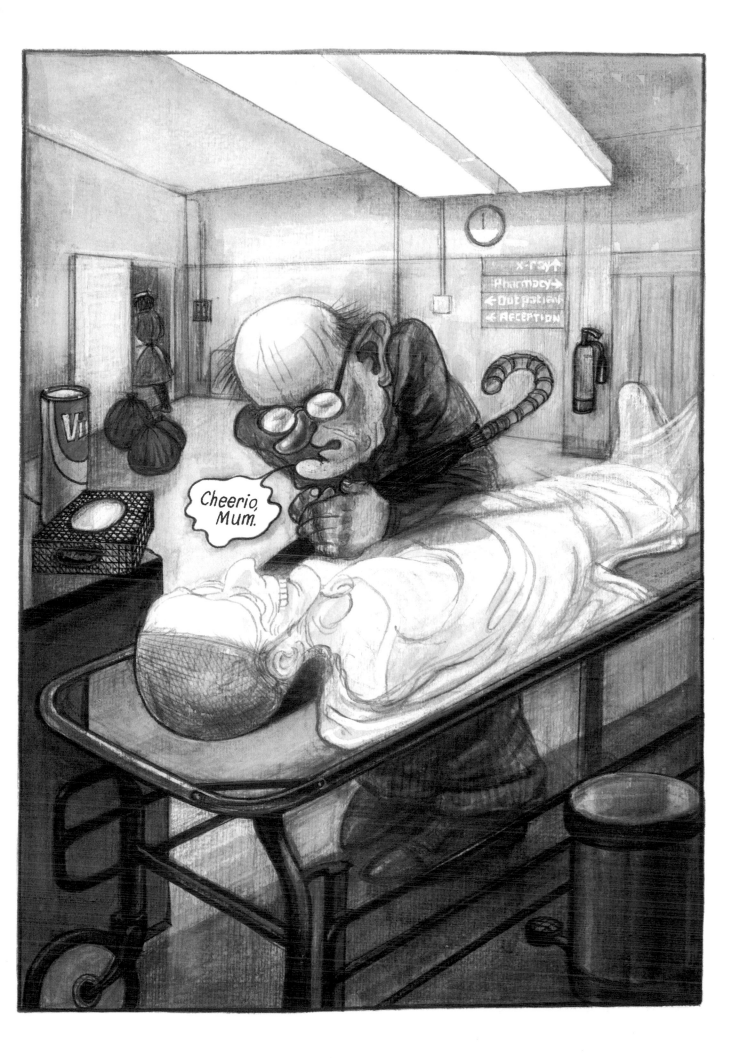

The following day Wally went to the hospital to collect his Mother's things. When he was handed her wedding ring in an envelope and her clothes in a black plastic dustbin sack, he fainted. In falling, he hit his head on the corner of a metal filing cabinet. The cut had to have three stitches put in it and Wally was at the hospital for most of the day.

In the bus, on the way home, the plastic sack split open and his Mother's knickers fell out onto the floor.

After his Mother's funeral, when the aunts and uncles had gone, Wally stood alone in the front room, not knowing quite what to do.

He was still wearing his new black suit and it seemed disrespectful to take it off too soon. What should he do with the rest of the day? He couldn't go to the pictures on the day of his Mother's funeral, could he? Would it be right to watch television, here in this room where she had lain ill for so long?

Just then a man came to cut the electricity off. Wally had been so busy with hospital visiting and funeral arrangements he had not noticed the warning letters.

That evening, he started to cook his egg and chips on an old Primus stove, dating from his Father's cycling days.

Unfortunately, he spilled the paraffin.

After the deaths of his parents, Wally became almost addicted to television. He hired a video-recorder and since then he has become a regular at the video library in his local fish and chip shop. He has already discovered, on a high shelf, the "Adult" section.

   He was amazed when he saw the pictures on the covers and even more amazed when he saw the films. He never knew such things were physically possible.

Later, Wally felt guilty about watching these films in the front room, surrounded by his Mother's precious ornaments, so he moved the television to the spare room.

However, Wally soon found that his amazement far outweighed any excitement and soon even the amazement wore off.

After a lifetime of innocence, Wally became bored with pornography in less than a fortnight.

Wally's favourite television programme is "Come Dancing" and his favourite style is the Latin American. Oh! The Tango! The Paso Doble! The Cha-Cha-Cha!

He imagines himself wearing bull-fighter's skin-tight satin trousers, a wide-open frilly shirt with balloon sleeves and an oily hair style with sideboards and curls.

Mavis is his partner, but a Mavis grown very tall, with delicately waving arms, a naked supple back and unbelievably long legs. Sequins glitter in her hair and her thighs flash amid a flurry of petticoats as she and Wally whirl and stamp to the throb of the passionate Mexican music. Oh!

Wally likes best the part where the man goes all stern and rigid and tosses the woman carelessly about like a flower.

Unfortunately, Wally cannot dance. He has tried several times with his aunties but he found it difficult to move his big feet in time to the music.

After his Mum died, Wally started using a laundry. The van called once a week and Wally used to leave the box in the porch. One week, the laundry man forgot to leave a box, so Wally put his washing out in a plastic bag. When the dustman espied the extra bag in the porch he snatched it up and flung it into the big grinder on the back of the lorry. It contained five of Wally's best shirts.

Wally saw this from his front room but could not get the window open in time.

One day it dawned on Wally that he was not getting any younger and he still had no experience of WOMEN.

What could be done? He asked an old colleague at work, Mr Blemkin, and Mr Blemkin told Wally about the cards in a certain newsagent's window. Wally reconnoitred the shop several times, striding along, very casually, whistling and gazing up at the sky as he passed.

Suppose someone saw? An aunty might be on a passing bus...an uncle might bob up from nowhere...his Mum, Up Above, might SEE in some mysterious, Heavenly way.

Eventually, Wally decided to be very discreet. He bought a coat and hat from the OXFAM shop and crept along at dusk, in disguise.

Once there, he quickly memorised a phone number and hurried away, red with shame, muttering it to himself over and over again, until he was far enough away to pause and scribble it on the palm of his hand.

It took him three weeks to summon up the courage to telephone and, when at last he got to the place, he was too frightened to do anything.

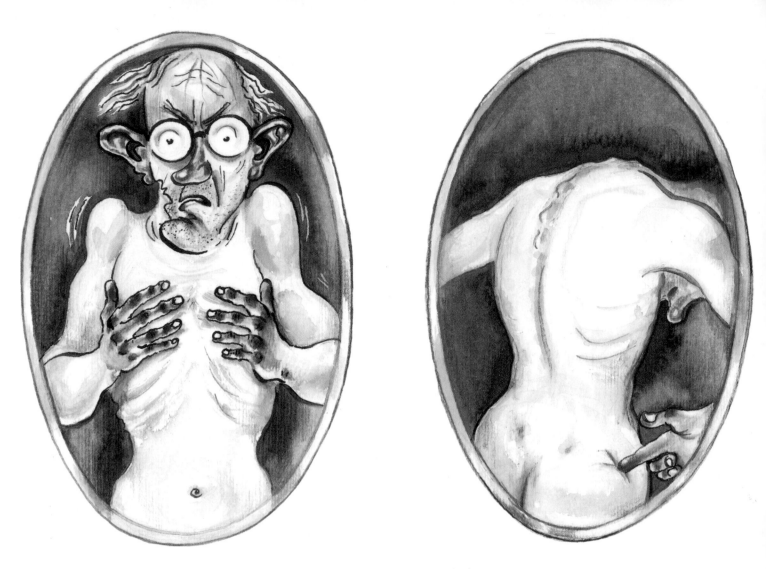

Also, surprisingly late in life, Wally began to hear about people called Homo-sexuals. At first, he refused to believe it, but gradually he came to realise it was "a fact of life in the Twentieth Century" as his Dad used to say.

Wally had never met one, as far as he knew, but then – how did you *know*? One day, an awesome thought struck Wally. *He* had never married and he had never had a girl friend...could it be that *he* was a Homo-sexual? Wally came out in a cold sweat. He did not want to be one. What would his Mum Up Above think? What did they look like?

That night he rushed home from work to look at himself in the mirror – naked. He felt his chest: no bosoms appearing there. He prodded his hips: no excessive fat or feminine curves there. He examined his private parts and decided there was no sign of Hermaphroditism (which he had seen a programme about). Perhaps it was all OK? Should he go to the Doctor for an examination? What about his hormones? How could you tell?

He started looking at men in the street to see if he found them attractive, but this proved to be unhelpful.

One day, as a scientific experiment, Wally bought a copy of both "Playboy" and "Playgirl" magazines. He turned their pages simultaneously to find which he responded to most. He discovered, with some relief, that he preferred the females, but he also found that he was not really all that bothered by either. So he decided, eventually, that he must be some kind of Neuter.

Why did people make so much fuss about it? he wondered. He still loved Mavis and longed to hold her in his arms and even to lie in bed with her, cuddling, but he never imagined taking her knickers off, let alone his own knickers as well and then – No! Impossible! Not with Mavis. It would be disrespectful.

Yet, suddenly the thought struck him that his Mum and Dad must have...done it. Mum and Dad! Surely not? But obviously they had, otherwise he wouldn't be here. *Some* time they had; years ago when they were young. It was almost unthinkable – his own Mother! Doing *that!*

Every single person on earth meant that two people had…done it, at least once, and for every birth there must be umpteen…Wally was appalled by this thought. People must be at it all the time! Otherwise there wouldn't *be* any people. Was he the only one *not* doing it? How did they find someone to do it with? But then, he didn't much want to do it anyway. Perhaps he *ought* to want to do it more? How often did they do it? Didn't married couples get *tired* of doing it, night after night, year after year? Surely it got boring; not to say…sore?

One night, after many hours of these tortuous thoughts, Wally fell asleep quite contented. He was not a Homo-sexual, he was sure of it. But he was equally sure he did not want to keep on and on doing *that* with some woman either.

He was all right as he was, with his dreams of Mavis and his memories of Mum. They were women enough for him.

As he grows older, Wally seems to become more and more like his Mother. He has even taken up knitting which was always his Mother's passion.

Wally has enough Mum-made pullovers to last him several life-times, so he knits other useful things instead. He has made four cushion covers for the front room, two tea cosies (one for every day and an extra nice one for Sundays), a jacket for his hot water bottle and several coat hangers, complete with dangling lavender bags.

Occasionally, Wally lays out all these handiworks together. The colour harmonies he has created fill him with pride and pleasure.

At Christmas time last year, Wally was made redundant. He had worked at the same family firm, doing much the same job, since he was sixteen. The company was run by his Uncle Joe, who had always had a soft spot for Wally and throughout his life referred to him as "the boy". When he was young Wally had resented this, but as he grew older he came to like it.

The firm had been manufacturing paper bags since 1919 and then, quite suddenly one day, it was "taken over". Right up until the end, Wally was still the youngest in the Accounts Department and he was treated as the office boy, even though he was forty-nine.

On their last day, the four men in the office held a farewell party. Wally thinks he drank an entire bottle of Dubonnet and two litres of Lemonade, but he really cannot remember.

Recently, Wally's hypochondria has taken the form of worry about growing old.
He even borrowed a book from the Public Library called "Easy-to-Make Aids to Help
the Aged".

Wally has always been interested in simple carpentry, though he has never had much
luck with it. Despite this, he has now started equipping himself for the onslaught of
Old Age, which he feels to be imminent.

He has made himself A Sloping Footrest, put his chair on A Trolley, made A Draught
Screen, A Shoe Remover, A Bedside Step, A Bread and Butter Spreader, A Bath
Trapeze Lift, and A Lavatory Wall Pull Handle.

The house is now so full of rickety wooden gadgets that it is quite a dangerous place.

Wally, now just fifty, is not particularly unhappy. He has recovered from the deaths of his Mother and Father and he only occasionally feels lonely.

Although he has daydreams of a life with his childhood sweetheart Mavis, he knows these are only daydreams.

His main ambition in life is to own a car: a red one, with a sunshine roof. He has just had another seventeen driving lessons and he is definitely improving.

Although Wally has very little money, he has no debts, the house is paid for and his funeral is insured. Also, apart from his lifelong hypochondria and his usual list of minor ailments, he is quite healthy. His Doctor died long ago.

There is no job to go to, no Dad to boss him, no Mum to embarrass him and no wife to nag him. Every day is his own. And every day he has a Dubonnet and Lemonade, with a cherry on a little stick.

All in all, he is not much unhappier than he ever was
and the future looks only a little worse than the past.

Wally considers himself quite lucky.